UoLear

Easy 4 me 2 learn

D1489919

## Bestselling books by Heather Baker

Successful Minute Taking, ISBN 978-1-84937-038-7

Successful Business Writing, ISBN 978-1-84937-071-4

Order books from your favourite bookseller or direct from www.uolearn.com

# Speedwriting Skills Training Course

## Speed writing for faster note taking and dictation, an alternative to shorthand to help you take notes

Easy exercises to learn faster writing in just 6 hours
Free downloadable Dictionary and Workbook

Published by: Universe of Learning Ltd, reg number 6485477, Lancashire, UK
www.UoLearn.com, support@UoLearn.com

Copyright © 2012 by Heather Baker,
The moral right of this author has been asserted.

First Published 2012

All rights reserved.  No part of this book may be reproduced either electronically or on paper without permission in writing from the publisher, except for passages of less than 500 words for purposes of review.

ISBN  978-1-84937-075-2

Other editions:
ebook pdf format 978-1-84937-009-7
ebook epub format 978-1-84937-010-3
Other imprints: American English spelling 978-1-84937-011-0

Universe of Learning and UoLearn are trademarks of Universe of Learning Ltd.

BakerWrite is a trademark of Baker Thompson Associates Ltd and is used with permission.

Photographs © www.fotolia.com
Cover photo © Avava, www.fotolia.com
Edited by Dr Margaret Greenhall.

The publisher and author assume no liability for any loss or damage, personal or otherwise which is directly or indirectly caused by the application of any of the contents of this book.

# **Contents**

| | Page |
|---|---|

# About the author

Heather had over twenty years' experience as a secretary and PA before setting up Baker Thompson Associates Limited in 2000. The company specialises in the training and development of secretarial and administrative staff, www.bakerthompsonassoc.co.uk.

She now travels all over the UK working with large and small companies to enable their office staff and PAs to work more effectively and efficiently. She also delivers courses in the Middle and Far East. Heather is a Certified NLP Practitioner.

She worked for ICI Pharmaceuticals (now AstraZeneca) and Hewlett Packard; she spent 5 years in France working for the Commercial Director of Cognac Hine and then 10 years with Granada Media working up to Personal Assistant to the Managing Director, commuting regularly between their offices in Manchester and London.

She developed this speed writing system to fulfil a requirement by many companies for a quick and easy way for their employees to take notes. The course became very popular and she was often asked if there was a book with the basics of the system – so here it is! This system is a top best seller on Amazon. BakerWrite speedwriting is also available to learn online at www.BakerWrite.com.

Heather is also the author of Successful Business Writing and Successful Minute Taking, available to order from any bookshop and at www. uolearn.com

Heather has been married to Ian since 1979 and they have two daughters, Ailsa and Erin. This book is dedicated to them with profound thanks for all their support over the years.

Have Fun!

# How did BakerWrite come into being?

When I was asked to teach speed writing (but not shorthand), I investigated various systems. All of those I researched seemed to have the same basics, which I also use; silent letters, omitting vowels, phonetic options, etc. However, it was the more advanced issues of prefixes and suffixes which seemed to me to be too complex.

I thought about the two shorthand systems with which I am familiar – Pitman and Teeline – and realised that I could use some of the techniques they employ, but still using letters. That is where the idea came from for the subscript and superscript.

I also thought that many people may feel restricted by rigid systems and so wanted to ensure that learners could feel they were able to adapt the method to suit their preferences. I offer guidelines rather than principles, suggestions rather than rules.

Best Wishes

Heather

# Praise for Heather and the BakerWrite system of speed writing

✓ "This was the best course I have ever attended."
"I learnt a lot and will be able to put it into practice straightaway."

✓ "The principles are very easy to follow, and I am already using it to take notes."

✓ "BakerWrite is the easiest shorthand system I have come across. Having studied all the major shorthand systems and even other speed writing courses, I find BakerWrite a sheer delight."

✓ "I feel that BakerWrite could be a complete shorthand system."
*Robbie, Glasgow*

✓ "Your system is so easy to learn and use." *Dawn, London*

✓ "I like the way the book is easy to carry around and it's so simple to understand." *Sue, Manchester*

✓ "The best things about this event were the enthusiasm of the teacher, the fact it was interactive and the helpful information. It was an excellent course; clear, concise and really enjoyable and I would recommend it to others. This course could not be improved, it was brill!"
*University of Salford*

✓ "The speed writing trainer was informative, relaxed and helpful. Excellent. She was very helpful, enthusiastic and approachable. She made the topic more fun and less scary. All the examples really helped and brought it to life."
*The Jockey Club*

✓ "The tutor was excellent – a thoroughly enjoyable day."
  *The Jockey Club*

✓ "I will recommend this course to everyone who takes notes."

✓ "Excellent course, well delivered – lots learned."

✓ "I thoroughly enjoyed the course."

✓ "My expectations were exceeded with this course."

✓ "Heather you are very helpful and supportive –
  excellent course."

✓ "Trainer was very helpful, friendly and informative and also
  very encouraging."

✓ "Heather had a way of relaxing/de-stressing all which
  enabled people to keep going and take it all in."

✓ "Tutor was very helpful and able to answer all questions.
  It was good having the person who
  invented the system to do the course."

✓ "Heather was patient and was more than able to
  answer our questions."

✓ "Heather is very friendly and the course was presented in an
  easy to understand way and at a good pace."

✓ "I liked the trainer's straightforward way of explaining the
  subject matter with the practical sessions."

✓ "Heather took the necessary time to answer questions and to
  ensure the group was happy and comfortable."

✓ "I will use this system all the time."

✓ "Used daily this system could have a major impact."

✓ "The training was exceptionally well delivered.  Heather was
  extremely helpful, patient and good humoured, even when
  being tested by some of the group!!"

✓ "A wonderful day – thank you v much."

# How to use this book

The book is laid out as six easy to follow guided hours, with lots of exercises. All the answers to the exercises are at the back of the book, along with a dictionary. The skill of speed writing is easy to learn. However, you do need to practise to get the full benefit of the course. The best way to use the book is to do one section, then practise for a few days then carry on with the next section.

As you develop your own abbreviations please do add them to the dictionary at the back of the book. We've left lots of space for you to do this or you can download a printable copy, with even more space to write in, from our website.

If you need help then can email us via support@UoLearn.com or you can visit the authors' section in www.UoLearn.com where you'll find a link for Heather.

The exercises in the book come with spaces to write, if it's your own book we invite you to do this. If you prefer, we have a free downloadable workbook with all the exercises in it in the 'Speed Writing' section of www.UoLearn.com

When you are making fast notes it is often from someone speaking so we've got some extra recorded exercises on the website too. Special thanks are given to Ailsa Baker for providing the voice for the dictations. Suggested answers for the dictations are available in the downloadable workbook. There is one dictation for each chapter and they are found on the website, www.Uolearn.com.

# First hour

# Silent letters and vowels

"Learning is a treasure that will follow its owner everywhere." Chinese Proverb

# First hour:
# Silent letters and vowels

In the first hour you will learn the basics of BakerWrite and you will have an opportunity to think about the abbreviations you already use when you are texting or taking notes quickly.

You will get some tips on how to practise BakerWrite to enable you to remember the abbreviations, and some tips on technique.

## The basics:

Things you probably already use:

| Abbreviation | Meaning |
|:---:|:---:|
| & | and |
| c | see, sea |
| i | I |
| r | are |
| u | you |
| y | why |
| 2 | two, to, too |
| 4 | four, for, fore |
| no | number |
| nb | note well |
| ie | that is |
| etc | and so on |
| eg | for example |

Let's add to that:

| Abbreviation | Meaning |
|:---:|:---:|
| s | is |
| t | it |
| f | of |
| b | be, being, been |
| m | me |
| w | we |
| v | very |
| hv | have |
| th | the* |

*You could also use a full stop instead of th for the and then use / for the end of a sentence.

**Notes:**

For very common words like 'of' we drop the initial vowel.

Where there is more than one meaning (e.g. b = be, being or been) then the context will make it clear which you want.

Also symbols:

| | |
|:---:|:---:|
| = | equals |
| ? | question, why |
| + | plus |
| < | less than |
| > | more than |
| ∴ | therefore |

And you probably have many more of your own.

In order to learn a new system of speed writing (or shorthand) it is vital to practise regularly and, unfortunately, only constant repetition will work.

You know how you learn all the jingles and products from the TV adverts because they are broadcast so often.

> **Exercise 1 : What abbreviations do you use?**
>
> Here's a blank table, add a few of your abbreviations to it.

| Abbreviation | Meaning |
|---|---|
|  |  |

**Top tips for practising:**

- ✓ At the end of each section of theory (as above) write the speed writing outline about 10 times while saying the word in your head (don't repeat the longhand – you know that!).

- ✓ Then dictate the words to a partner or put them onto a tape recorder and play them back to take them as dictation. This is important as it replicates the work situation. You need to be able to react quickly when you hear a word to build up speed.

- ✓ Reading is OK sometimes, but it is important to build up your ability to hear the word and write it quickly; you won't do this by reading only.

- ✓ Always write the words across the page, not down, as you would if you were taking notes.

- ✓ When you're drilling new groups of words, keep reminding yourself of words you drilled earlier.

- ✓ Don't copy from the book. Look at the abbreviation once and then write it from memory.

- ✓ Always use lower case – capital letters really slow you down. Use handwriting rather than printing, unless you usually print. This system is intended to make your life easier, not more difficult! If you find a particular combination of letters difficult to write, often you may write that combination in another word – think how you join them there (for example, some people find writing ltl for little a bit awkward; see how you write l and t in the words bolt or halt).

- ✓ Also make your writing small and close together and don't press too hard with your pen or pencil – you will become very tired.

- ✓ You should use acronyms wherever possible (e.g. nhs, bbc).

With that in mind, I must reiterate that these are only guidelines not rules; if there is some part of the system you don't like, then don't use it, but do find an alternative that suits you. As long as it creates a shorter version of the word or phrase then it should be fine.

So have a go first of all at drilling the list of abbreviations from above.

**Space for you to practise:**

# Silent letters:

> *Omit all silent letters – just write what you hear.*

A good example of this of this is 'i c u' for I see you.

| Abbreviation | Meaning |
|---|---|
| no | know |
| tl | tell, till |
| scs | success |
| btr | better |
| ltl | little |
| cf | cough |

**Notes:**

In 'know' we don't pronounce the k or the w and we'll talk more about vowels next.

With words like till and tell remember the context will make it clear when you are writing in sentences.

Words can be written phonetically too, like cough.

---

Exercise 2 : Drill the words then speed write:

1.  I see the butter.

2.  We have success.

3.  I have very little.

And remember some other familiar abbreviations:

| Abbreviation | Meaning |
|:---:|:---:|
| mbr | member |
| dpt | department |
| org | organised organisation |
| mtg | meeting |
| mkt | market |

Here are some ways to differentiate between common, similar words:

| | |
|:---:|:---:|
| tn | than |
| tht | that |
| thr | their, there, they're |
| thm | them |
| thn | then |
| ths | these |
| thy | they |
| thi | this |
| thos | those |
| | |
| wr | were |
| wh | what |
| whn | when |
| whr | where |
| whl | while |
| wl | will |
| wi | with |
| w/in | within |
| w/ou | without |

## Vowels:

> *Leave out vowels unless you need*
> *them to clarify your meaning.*

| Abbreviation | Meaning |
|--------------|-----------|
| md | mad |
| sl | sell, sill |
| bt | bet |
| fl | fill |
| clr | collar |
| bg | bug |

> *Also for clarity you could include just long vowels, i.e. you*
> *don't have a vowel for sell*
> *or fill but you do for seal or file.*

| | |
|----------|--------|
| mad (md) | made |
| bet | beat |
| sel | seal |
| fil | file |
| col | coal |
| bugl | bugle |
| vlu | value |

Exercise 3 : Drill the words then speed write:

1. The file is full.
2. We know the value of the file.
3. I sell at the market.

Exercise 4 : What would you use for the following words?

| Abbreviation | Meaning |
|---|---|
| | hello |
| | dear |
| | yours |
| | please |
| | feel |
| | try |
| | book |
| | address |

You may also want to include vowels (long or short) if you feel there may be some ambiguity of meaning. Often the context makes it clear what your abbreviated word means, but occasionally it may not be obvious; we will look at this later.

You may also occasionally want to add other letters for clarity. We use "no" for no, know, number and November; if you feel you may get confused you could use "no" for no and know, "num" or "#" for number and "nov" for November.

> *However, having suggested you miss out vowels wherever possible, there is one place you should always use them, and that is at the beginning of a word.*

If I were to write "nspr" I would probably assume the word begins with an n. In fact I wanted to write inspire. If I write "inspr" it is immediately clear what the word is.
Some other words to drill:

| Abbreviation | Meaning |
|:---:|:---:|
| if | if |
| efct | effect |
| afct | affect |
| acpt | accept |

> However, where a word begins ex you don't need to include the e as that clearly should be there:

| xtnsv | extensive |
|:---:|:---:|
| xmpl | example |
| xcpt | except |

**Exercise 5 : Drill the words then do the sentences below:**

1. I have an extensive effect on the class.
2. It is mad to work for other people.
3. Organisation is the key to success.

................................................................

................................................................

................................................................

## Exercise 6 : First hour summary exercises

1. Do you accept my view is better?
2. I bet you beat the eggs.
3. Please accept this free sample.
4. You know he sells files.
5. The department had success.
6. It is better to seal the file.
7. The value of the meeting is better.
8. Go to the market for value.
9. Except for me, the group knows you.
10. A little success is very good.

1

2

3

4

5

6

7

8

9

10

Once you've finished each hour remember to visit
www.UoLearn.com where you'll find an audio exercise.

# Second hour

# Phonetics and prefixes

"I didn't have time to write a short letter, so I wrote a long one instead." Mark Twain

# Second hour:
# Phonetics and prefixes

In the second hour we continue with further options. Some of these are definitely not obligatory. They involve some phonetic options – that is when words look like they sound, rather than how they are written.

We also introduce the use of subscript characters. This means we drop a character below the line to represent a commonly used group of letters.

You will get some tips on preparing for note-taking situations.

We then move on to prefixes. Prefixes are common beginnings to words. For these we use superscript characters; this means we raise a character above the word (like using quotation marks) to represent common prefixes.

# Phonetic options:

> *Some people like to use more phonetic ways of writing.*
> *If you do then you may like to try these examples,*
> *if not just use the usual letters.*

---

*Use a k for the letter k and also for a hard c:*

| Abbreviation | Meaning |
|---|---|
| k (cn) | can |
| kd (cd) | could |
| kas (cas or cs) | case |
| klnk (clnc) | clinic |

The non-phonetic version is in brackets.

---

*However, you should always use a k to replace ck:*

| bk | back |
|---|---|
| lk | lock |

---

*For a soft c, continue to use c:*

| ces | cease |
|---|---|
| cntr | centre |

> *You could also use a j for the letter j and for soft g:*

| Abbreviation | Meaning |
|---|---|
| aj (ag) | age |
| mnj (mng) | manage |
| jj (jg) | judge* |
| klj (clg) | college |

*In words like judge we don't really pronounce the d.

> *Some other ways of reducing your writing is by using 2 letters instead of 3 for abbreviations for months and days:*

| | |
|---|---|
| ja | January |
| fe | February |
| ma | March |
| ap | April |
| my | May |
| ju | June |
| jl | July |
| au | August |
| se | September |
| oc | October |
| no | November |
| de | December |
| mo | Monday |
| tu | Tuesday |
| we | Wednesday |
| th | Thursday |
| fr | Friday |
| sa | Saturday |
| su | Sunday |

Exercise 7 : Drill all the new words, then try this:

1. I can carry the case back to the centre.
2. Can you manage to get the judge to the college?

Exercise 8 : What would you use for the following words?

| Abbreviation | Meaning |
|---|---|
| | hedge |
| | tick |
| | track |
| | clear |
| | desk |
| | link |
| | candle |
| | second |
| | crisp |
| | cell |
| | lucky |
| | piece |
| | fudge |

Next we are going to introduce the use of subscript and superscript.

> *First of all we are going to use a subscript c $_{(c)}$ to represent the letters ch or tch:*

| Abbreviation | Meaning |
|:---:|:---:|
| $e_c$ | each |
| $t_c$ | touch |
| $te_c$ | teach |
| $_ck$ | check |
| $_cq$ | cheque |
| $f_c$ | fetch |
| $w_c$ | watch or which |

Your brain tells you that you can't do this as for many years you have always written a c on the line – keep practising, it will become easier.

> *If you want to abbreviate even more, you could also use subscript t $_{(t)}$ for th, and s $_{(s)}$ for sh. etc,*

| | |
|:---:|:---:|
| $c_s$ | cash |
| $_swr$ | shower |
| $_tnk$ | think |
| $o_tr$ | other |

Again, this is optional.

> **Exercise 9 :** Drill those words and then try the dictation.
> It may feel strange at first but you will get used to it.
>
> 1. Pay for the book.
> 2. Give me a cheque for the bill.
> 3. The book is big.
> 4. Can I see the bell?
> 5. Can I have the value of the new book?

## Top tips:

✓ When you are going to take notes in meetings or dictation, it is always a good idea to have practised your abbreviations as much as possible beforehand. One of the reasons people can't read back their notes is because they make up abbreviations during meetings and then can't remember what they meant.

✓ If you've prepared in advance you will know what to write and what your abbreviation means. You can add to the dictionary at the end of the book or download a printable copy from www.UoLearn.com.

✓ Think also about people's initials, departments in your organisation, products and/or services.
How could you abbreviate these? When you have finished this book, you will have all the knowledge you need to start making up your own abbreviations. More of this later....

✓ Use a Livescribe smartpen to take notes. This computer in a pen records everything you write, hear or say.
(http://www.bakerwrite.com/cms/tools).

# Prefixes:

We're now going to look at some examples of prefixes. A prefix is found at the beginning of a word and the abbreviations we will use are for the very common prefixes.

*We're going to use a superscript c $^{(c)}$ for the prefixes con and com:*

| Abbreviation | Meaning |
|---|---|
| $^c$sdr | consider |
| $^c$pr | compare |
| $^c$plx | complex |
| $^c$mty | community |
| $^c$tmpry | contemporary |
| $^c$slt | consult |
| $^c$tct | contact |
| $^c$plint | compliant |
| $^c$plant | complaint |

*Use a superscript d $^{(d)}$ for des and dis:*

| | |
|---|---|
| $^d$pr | despair |
| $^d$ma | dismay |
| $^d$apr | disappear |
| $^d$aprv | disapprove |
| $^d$prv | disprove |

Exercise 10 : Drill those words and then do this exercise:

1.  I despair of you.
2.  We contact the clinic.
3.  Could you consider the effect.

Space for you to practise:

## Exercise 11 : Second hour summary exercises

1. The community considers each case.
2. I was dismayed at the lack of success.
3. The other cheque was lost.
4. Consult the judge each day.
5. He disappeared to teach the class.
6. Did you consider each complaint?
7. Can you manage to compare the centres?
8. I fetched the watch back from the clinic.
9. Could you cease, please.
10. How much cash do you have?

1

2

3

4

5

6

7

8

9

10

Remember to go to www.UoLearn.com for your hour 2 dictation exercise and downloadable workbook.

# Third hour
# More prefixes

"Our greatest weakness lies in giving up.
The most certain way to succeed is always to
try just one more time." Thomas Edison

# Third hour: More prefixes

In this hour we continue with some more examples of superscript characters being used for common prefixes.

> *Use a superscript f $^{(f)}$ or a 4 for the prefix for and fore:*

| Abbreviation | | Meaning |
|:---:|:---:|:---:|
| $^f$tl | 4tl | foretell |
| $^f$cst | 4cst | forecast |
| $^f$wrn | 4wrn | forewarn |
| $^f$nm | 4nm | forename |

**Top tip:**

✓ Be very careful to make the f clearly superscript, otherwise it will just look like a capital letter and may confuse you. Also, decide which version you prefer and stick to that. If you keep changing this could make your transcriptions more difficult.

> *Use a superscript i $^{(i)}$ for inter and intro:*

| | |
|---|---|
| $^i$m | interim |
| $^i$rpt | interrupt |
| $^i$dc | introduce |
| $^i$vw | interview |
| $^i$nt | internet |

**Top tip:**

✓ If you prefer not to dot the i that will speed things up too.

---

Exercise 12 : When you have drilled those new words, have a go at the following sentences:

1. Introduce me to the judge.
2. We could foretell the extensive damage.
3. We interrupt the meeting to check the lock.

> *Use a superscript p $^{(p)}$ for pro, per, pre:*

| Abbreviation | Meaning |
|---|---|
| $^p$pr | prepare |
| $^p$fct | perfect |
| $^p$mt | permit |
| $^p$vd | provide |
| $^p$psl | proposal |
| $^p$tct | protect |
| $^p$mot | promote |
| $^p$dct | product |

| | |
|---|---|
| *Use a superscript s $^{(s)}$ for sub, sup or super:* | |

| | |
|---|---|
| $^s$mt | submit |
| $^s$prs | suppress |
| $^s$mkt | supermarket |
| $^s$prt | support |

**Exercise 13 :  Practise the new words, then try this:**

1.   We provide the supermarket at the centre.
2.  The success of this project may compare well.
3.  The supermarket sells big books.

**Exercise 14 :  What would you use for these words?**

| Abbreviation | Meaning |
|---|---|
| | fortune |
| | prefer |
| | programme |
| | introvert |
| | interfere |
| | supervise |
| | substitute |

Space for you to practise:

## Exercise 15 : Third hour summary exercises

1. Your forename is on the internet.
2. The forecast for the company is excellent.
3. Their interim figures are prepared and in the proposal.
4. Which supermarket do you visit?
5. I submit my proposal for the interview.
6. She interrupts me when I am at my desk.
7. Are you prepared to provide good value?
8. He protects his child from harm.
9. The product is introduced by the manager.
10. Consult the interim paper as soon as possible.

1

2

3

4

5

6

7

8

9

10

Your free hour 3 audio exercise is waiting for you at www.UoLearn.com.

# Fourth hour

# Extra prefix ideas

"There is no happiness except in the realisation
that we have accomplished something."
Henry Ford

# Fourth hour: Extra prefixes

In this hour we will finish the prefixes.

*Use a superscript t $^{(t)}$ for trans:*

| Abbreviation | Meaning |
|---|---|
| $^{t}$prt | transport |
| $^{t}$fr | transfer |
| $^{t}$mt | transmit |

*Use a superscript u $^{(u)}$ for under:*

| | |
|---|---|
| $^{u}$nth | underneath |
| $^{u}$stnd | understand |
| $^{u}$ | under |

*Use a superscript m $^{(m)}$ for multi:*

| | |
|---|---|
| $^{m}$stry | multi-storey |
| $^{m}$pl | multiple |

You will see that we have not used all the alphabet. That is because this system is very flexible and you can adapt it to your needs. You may prefer to use m for mega or any other prefix that would help you.

You could use two letters for longer prefixes, for example, $^{ac}$ for accomm or $^{rc}$ for recomm. $^{pp}$ could be used for propor.

In the NHS people use $^{a}$ for audio, $^{h}$ and $_{h}$ for hyper and hypo.

Have a think about what would help you. However, don't worry too much about words for which you already have abbreviations – stick with these; this system is meant to help you, not confuse you!

---

**Exercise 16 :  Some final dictation on prefixes to try, when you have drilled the latest group of words:**

1.  He tells me the transport is in the multi-storey car park.
2.  Do you understand the transfer must be made to provide the funds?

---

## Exercise 17 : Fourth hour summary exercises

1. Please transmit the letters by email.
2. I understand you provide an excellent service.
3. The transfer was underneath the minimum amount.
4. Complaints have been received each week.
5. Multi-media is new this century.
6. The internet transmits data immediately.
7. He translates the documents from Spanish into English.
8. Do not underestimate the Chief Executive.
9. We recommend the member pays his fees.
10. It is not easy to accommodate students.

1

2

3

4

5

6

7

8

9

10

Have a look on the website (www.UoLearn.com) for the hour 4 exercise.

# Fifth hour
# Suffixes

"Nobody can go back and start a new beginning, but anyone can start today and make a new ending."
Maria Robinson

# Fifth hour:
# Suffixes

Now we start to look at suffixes. Suffixes are common endings to words and, as for the prefixes, we will use a superscript character to represent a group of letters that make up some of the common suffixes.

> *We're going to use the superscript b $^{(b)}$*
> *for the suffixes ible and able:*

| Abbreviation | Meaning |
|---|---|
| $t^b$ | table |
| $ps^b$ | possible |
| $acs^b$ | accessible |
| $avl^b$ | available |
| $rspn^b$ | responsible |
| $^b$ | able |

and we can use prefixes and suffixes to **really** save time

| | |
|---|---|
| $^csdr^b$ | considerable |
| $^cfrt^b$ | comfortable |
| $^pb^{by}$ | probably, probability |

*Use a superscript f $^{(f)}$ for the suffix ful:*

| Abbreviation | Meaning |
|---|---|
| hlp$^f$ | helpful |
| jy$^f$ | joyful |
| scs$^{fy}$ | successfully |

*Use superscript g $^{(g)}$ for ing:*

| | |
|---|---|
| wrk$^g$ | working |
| shp$^g$ | shopping |
| vst$^g$ | visiting |
| dr$^g$ | during |
| d$^g$ | doing |

You may not always just drop vowels; sometimes using the first 2 or 3 letters of a word can give a better clue :

| | |
|---|---|
| inc$^g$ | including |
| org$^g$ | organising |
| dev$^g$ | developing |

| Use superscript s $^{(s)}$ for cial/sial/tial: | |
| :--- | :--- |

| Abbreviation | Meaning |
| :---: | :---: |
| so$^s$ | social |
| rsdn$^s$ | residential |
| ptn$^s$ | potential |
| sp$^s$ | special |
| spa$^s$ | spatial* |
| sp$^{st}$ | specialist |

*Spatial is an example of where it is useful to put in the long vowel.

**Exercise 18 :  Practise the new words, then try this:**

1.  The teaching has the potential to affect all students.
2.  Our specialist services extend during the day.

Exercise 19 : Some words using the ideas in the fourth and fifth hours.

| Abbreviation | Meaning |
|---|---|
| | transaction |
| | transform |
| | underestimate |
| | multicultural |
| | incredible |
| | permissible |
| | connectable |
| | cheerful |
| | mixing |
| | commercial |

Space for you to practise:

## Exercise 20 : Fifth hour summary exercises

1. The new employee has great potential.
2. Is it possible to provide specialist tables?
3. Her social skills are lacking.
4. The successful meeting lasted two hours.
5. During the interview he considered her replies.
6. In all probability, it will be working by Friday.
7. Are you available for organising the department?
8. She is doing all she can to make people comfortable.
9. Accessibility is important to this company.
10. Your work has increased considerably.

1 ......................................................................................................

2 ......................................................................................................

3 ......................................................................................................

4 ......................................................................................................

5 ......................................................................................................

6 ......................................................................................................

7 ......................................................................................................

8 ......................................................................................................

9 ......................................................................................................

10 ......................................................................................................

Have a go now at the dictation for hour 5 at www.UoLearn.com.

# Sixth hour
# More suffixes

"The key is not in spending time but in investing it."
Stephen Covey

# Sixth hour:
# More suffixes

| Use superscript m $^{(m)}$ for ment: |
| :---: |

| Abbreviation | Meaning |
| :---: | :---: |
| pa$^m$ | payment |
| invl$^m$ | involvement |
| $^c$mt$^m$ | commitment |
| dev$^m$ | development |
| env$^m$ | environment |
| dtr$^{ml}$ | detrimental |
| fnd$^{my}$ | fundamentally |

| Use superscript c $^{(c)}$ for nce: |
| :---: |

| s$^c$ | since |
| :---: | :---: |
| $^c$fr$^c$ | conference |

| Use superscript p $^{(p)}$ for ship: |
| :---: |

| ldr$^p$ | leadership |
| :---: | :---: |
| mbr$^p$ | membership |
| rla$^{np}$ | relationship |

*Use superscript n $^{(n)}$ for sion/tion/cean:*

| Abbreviation | Meaning |
|---|---|
| sta$^n$ | station |
| sta$^{ny}$ | stationery |
| | stationary |
| m$^n$ | mission |
| $^c$m$^n$ | commission |
| $^c$ple$^n$ | completion |
| edu$^n$ | education |
| edu$^{nl}$ | educational |
| o$^n$ | ocean |
| $^i$n$^{nl}$ | international |
| $^s$v$^n$ | supervision |

As with the prefixes, you can use any other letters for suffixes that are useful for you. You could use, in a medical environment, $^i$ for itis, or in education use $^o$ for ology.

One final tip, many words used in business are compound words, ie, one word made up of two words. For example, spreadsheet, broadband, lifestyle, portfolio. A good way to write these quickly is to use a / giving you s/s, b/b, l/s, p/f. Think of some examples in your working life.

---

**Exercise 21 : Practise the new words, then try this:**

1. My involvement in the expansion of the company was useful.
2. Any hardship will be taken into account.

---

Exercise 22 : Using the ideas from the sixth hour, what are your abbreviations for the following?

| Abbreviation | Meaning |
|---|---|
| | contentment |
| | statement |
| | once |
| | ambulance |
| | existence |
| | fellowship |
| | connection |
| | foundation |

Exercise 23 : What other syllables do you use frequently? Add to this table.

| Abbreviation | Meaning |
|---|---|
| | ous |
| | ness |
| | anti/ante |
| | mis |
| | ivity |
| | less |
| | |
| | |
| | |

Space for you to practise:

## Exercise 24 : Sixth hour summary exercises

1. Transcription of speed writing is easy when you practise.
2. International supervision is vital to large companies.
3. It is fundamentally the hardship which causes problems.
4. Is your relationship with your team improving?
5. Their commitment is vital to the continuation of the business.
6. The organisation's mission covers education and the environment.
7. Membership of this club is very difficult.
8. His involvement with the commission took up a lot of time.
9. Is her behaviour detrimental to our department?
10. Our conference will be during the week.

1

2

3

4

5

6

7

8

9

10

Well done, your final exercise is at www.UoLearn.com.

# Action plan

"I'm a great believer in luck and
I find the harder I work, the more I have of it."
Thomas Jefferson

**Top tips:**

You have now learnt the basics of BakerWrite but you need to continue to work on this skill to become adept. These are some thoughts that may help you.

✓ Get yourself an A-Z notebook and enter in it all the new words you have learnt so far or download the printable dictionary from www.UoLearn.com. This is a good way to revise the theory you've learnt and provides you with your own personalised BakerWrite dictionary.

✓ Next you should start to think about the words and phrases you need for your area of work and put these in your new dictionary with the BakerWrite equivalents.

✓ Start to introduce BakerWrite into your every day life, but start gradually. A good idea is to begin by using the $^g$ for ing then, after a couple of days introduce another prefix or suffix.

✓ Use more and more of the abbreviated words and symbols.

✓ Regularly go through the theory and drill any words that cause you problems.

✓ Get yourself informed. When you are going to take notes at a meeting or are expecting calls on a particular topic, anticipate what vocabulary you may need and work out the BakerWrite version for them, put them in your dictionary and drill them. In this way you will have a structure to work with.

✓ Visit either Heather's website www.bakerthompsonassoc.co.uk or the publisher's website www.UoLearn.com for any BakerWrite updates and to network with other users.

✓ Finally, don't put yourself under too much pressure. It does take time to become proficient so don't become stressed if you can't take notes quickly straightaway. However, do be tenacious. Don't give in – keep at it.

Gd Lk!

| My action plan: |
| --- |

| Date | Action |
| --- | --- |
|  |  |

ACTION PLAN

| Date | Action |
|------|--------|
|      |        |

# Answers to the exercises

"I have to exercise in the morning before my brain figures out what I'm doing." Marsha Doble

# Answers to the exercises:

These are suggested ways you could write the exercises. They aren't the only way and as you work with the BakerWrite speed writing system and you'll develop your own style.

## Exercise 1 :

Your own choices.

## Exercise 2 :

1.  i c th btr.

2.  w hv scs.

3.  i hv v ltl.

## Exercise 3 :

1.  th fil s fl.

2.  w no th vlu f th fil.

3.  i sl @ th mkt.

## Exercise 4 :

| Abbreviation | Meaning |
|---|---|
| hlo | hello |
| dr | dear |
| yrs | yours |
| pls | please |
| fel | feel |
| try | try |
| bk | book |
| adrs | address |

## Exercise 5 :

1.  i hv a xtnsv efct on th cls

2.  t s md 2 wrk 4 othr ppl

3.  org s th ky 2 scs.

## Exercise 6 :

1.  do u acpt my vw s btr?

2.  i bt u bet th egs.

3.  pls acpt thi fre smpl.

4.  u no h sls fils.

5.  th dpt hd scs.

6.  t s btr 2 sel th fil.

7.  th vlu f th mtg s btr.

8.  go 2 th mkt 4 vlu.

9.  xcpt 4 m, th grp nos u.

10. a ltl scs s v gd.

## Exercise 7 :

1.  i k kry th kas bk 2 th cntr

2.  k u mnj 2 gt th jj 2 th klj?

## Exercise 8 :

| Abbreviation | Meaning |
|---|---|
| hj | hedge |
| tk | tick |
| trk | track |
| klr | clear |
| dsk | desk |
| lnk | link |
| kndl | candle |
| sknd (2nd) | second |
| krsp | crisp |
| cl | cell |
| lky | lucky |
| pec | piece |
| fj | fudge |

## Exercise 9 :

1. py 4 th bk.

2. gv m a $_c$q 4 th bl.

3. th bk s bg.

4. k i c th bl?

5. k i hv th vlu f th nw bk?

## Exercise 10 :

1. i $^d$pr f u.

2. w $^c$tct th klnk.

3. kd u $^c$sdr th efct.

## Exercise 11 :

1. th $^c$mnty $^c$sdrs e$_c$ kas.

2. i ws $^d$myd @ th lk f scs.

3. th o$_t$r $_c$q ws lst.

4. $^c$slt th jj e$_c$ da.

5. h $^d$aprd 2 te$_c$ th kls.

6. dd u $^c$sdr e$_c$ $^c$plant?

7. k u mnj 2 $^c$pr th cntrs?

8. i f$_{cd}$ th w$_c$ bk frm th klnk.

9. kd u ces, pls.

10. hw m$_c$ c$_s$ do u hv?

## Exercise 12 :

1. $^i$dc m 2 th jj.

2. w kd $^f$tl th xtnsv dmj.

3. w $^i$rpt th mtg 2 $_c$k th lk.

## Exercise 13 :

1. w $^p$vd th $^s$mkt @ th cntr.

2. th scs f thi $^p$jct ma $^c$pr wl.

3. th $^s$mkt sls bg bks.

## Exercise 14 :

| Abbreviation | Meaning |
|---|---|
| ᶠtun (4tun) | fortune |
| ᵖfr | prefer |
| ᵖgrm | programme |
| ⁱvr | introvert |
| ⁱfr | interfere |
| ˢvs | supervise |
| ˢstt | substitute |

## Exercise 15 :

1.  yr ᶠnm s on th ⁱnt.

2.  th ᶠcst 4 th co s xclnt.

3.  thr ⁱm figs r ᵖprd & in th ᵖpsl.

4.  w_c ˢmkt do u vst?

5.  i ˢmt my ᵖpsl 4 th ⁱvw.

6.  ₛe ⁱrpts m wn i am @ my dsk.

7.  r u ᵖprd 2 ᵖvd gd vlu?

8.  h ᵖtcts hs _cld frm hrm.

9.  th ᵖdct s ⁱdcd by th mnjr.

10. ᶜslt th ⁱm ppr asap.

## Exercise 16 :

1. h tls m th ᵗprt s in th ᵐstry kp.

2. do u ᵘstnd th ᶠfr mst b md 2 ᵖvd th fnds?

## Exercise 17 :

1. pls ᵗmt th ltrs by eml.
2. i ᵘstnd u ᴾvd a xclnt srvc.
3. th ᵗfr ws ᵘnth th min amnt.
4. ᶜplants hv b rcvd e$_c$ wk.
5. ᵐmed s nw thi cntry.
6. th ⁱnt ᵗmts data immed.
7. h ᵗlts th docs frm spn$_s$ in2 engl$_s$.
8. do nt ᵘest th ce.
9. w ʳᶜmnd th mbr pas hs fes.
10. t s nt esy 2 ᵃᶜmdt stdnts.

## Exercise 18 :

1. th t$_c$ᵍ hs th ptnˢ 2 afct al stdnts.
2. our spˢᵗ srvcs xtnd drᵍ th da.

**Exercise 19 :**

| Abbreviation | Meaning |
|---|---|
| $^t$ac$^n$ | transaction |
| $^{tf}$m | transform |
| $^u$est | underestimate |
| $^m$cul | multicultural |
| incrd$^b$ | incredible |
| $^p$ms$^b$ | permissible |
| $^c$nct$^b$ | connectable |
| $_c$r$^f$ | cheerful |
| mx$^g$ | mixing |
| $^c$mr$^s$ | commercial |

**Exercise 20 :**

1. th nw emplye hs gr8 ptn$^s$.

2. s t ps$^b$ 2 $^p$vd sp$^{st}$ t$^{bs}$?

3. hr so$^s$ skls r lk$^g$.

4. th scs$^f$ mtg lstd 2 hrs.

5. dr$^g$ th $^i$vw h $^c$sdrd hr rplis.

6. in al $^p$b$^{by}$ t wl b wrk$^g$ by fr.

7. r u avl$^b$ 4 org$^g$ th dpt?

8. $_s$e s d$^g$ al $_s$e k 2 mk ppl $^c$frt$^b$.

9. acs$^{by}$ s imp 2 thi co.

10. yr wrk hs incrsd $^c$sdr$^{by}$.

## Exercise 21 :

1. my invl$^m$ in th xpn$^n$ f th co ws us$^f$.

2. ny hrd$^p$ wl b tkn in2 acc.

## Exercise 22 :

| Abbreviation | Meaning |
|---|---|
| $^c$tnt$^m$ | contentment |
| stt$^m$ | statement |
| o$^c$ | once |
| amb$^c$ | ambulance |
| xst$^c$ | existence |
| flw$^p$ | fellowship |
| $^c$nct$^n$ | connection |
| fnd$^s$ | foundation |

## Exercise 23 :

Your own choices.

## Exercise 24 :

1. $^t$crp$^n$ f s/w$^g$ s esy wen u prcts.

2. $^i$n$^{nl}$ $^s$v$^n$ s vtl 2 lrj cos.

3. t s fnda$^{my}$ th hrd$^p$ w$_c$ css $^p$blms.

4. s yr rla$^{np}$ wi yr tem imprv$^g$?

5. thr $^c$mt$^m$ s vtl 2 th $^c$tnu$^n$ f th bus.

6. th org's m$^n$ cvrs edu$^n$ & th env$^m$.

7. mbr$^p$ f thi clb s v dfclt.

8. hs invlv$^m$ wi th $^c$m$^n$ tk up a lt f tm.

9. s hr bhvior dtri$^{ml}$ 2 our dpt?

10. our $^c$fr$^c$ wl b dr$^g$ th wk.

Space for you to practise:

# Speed Writing
# Dictionary

"Do not say a little in many words but a
great deal in a few." Pythagorus

| A | |
|---|---|
| able | b |
| accept | acpt |
| accessible | acs[b] |
| accommodate | [ac]mdt |
| account | acc |
| affect | afct |
| age | aj |
| all | al |
| amount | amnt |
| an | a |
| and | & |
| and so on | etc |
| any | ny |
| are | r |
| as soon as possible | asap |
| at | @ |
| available | avl[b] |

| B | |
|---|---|
| back | bk |
| be | b |
| beat | bet |
| behaviour | bhvr |
| bell | bl |
| bet | bt |
| better | btr |
| big | bg |
| bill | bl |
| book | bk |
| bug | bg |
| bugle | bugl |
| business | bus |
| butter | btr |

| C | |
|---|---|
| can | k / cn |
| carry | kry / cry |
| case | kas / cas |
| cash | $c_s/k_s$ |
| causes | css /kss |
| cease | ces |
| centre | cntr |
| century | cntry |
| check | $_ck$ |
| cheque | $_cq$ |
| child | $_cld$ |
| class | kls / cls |
| clinic | klnk |
| club | klb / clb |
| coal | kol / col |
| collar | klr / clr |
| college | klj/clg/clj |
| comfortable | $^cfrt^b$ |
| commission | $^cm^n$ |
| commitment | $^cmt^m$ |
| community | $^cmty$ |
| company | co |
| compare | $^cpr$ |
| complaint | $^cplant$ |
| completion | $^cple^n$ |
| complex | $^cplx$ |
| compliant | $^cplint$ |
| conference | $^cfr^c$ |

| C | |
|---|---|
| consider | $^csdr$ |
| considerable | $^csdr^b$ |
| consult | $^cslt$ |
| contact | $^ctct$ |
| contemporary | $^ctmpry$ |
| continuation | $^ctnu^n$ |
| cough | kf / cf |
| could | kd / cd |
| covers | kvrs/cvrs |

| D | |
|---|---|
| damage | dmj |
| data | dta |
| day | da |
| department | dpt |
| desk | dsk |
| despair | $^d$pr |
| detrimental | dtr$^{ml}$ |
| development | dev$^m$ |
| did | dd |
| difficult | dif |
| disappear | $^d$apr |
| disapprove | $^d$aprv |
| dismay | $^d$ma |
| disprove | $^d$prv |
| do | do |
| document | doc |
| doing | d$^g$ |
| during | dr$^g$ |

| E | |
|---|---|
| each | e$_c$ |
| easy | esy |
| educational | edu$^{nl}$ |
| effect | efct |
| email | eml |
| employee | emplye |
| English | engl$_s$ |
| environment | env$^m$ |
| equals | = |
| example | xmpl |
| excellent | xclnt |
| except | xcpt |
| expansion | xpn$^n$ |
| extend | xtnd |
| extensive | xtnsv |

| F | |
|---|---|
| fees | fes |
| fetch | $f_c$ |
| figures | fgrs/figs |
| file | fil |
| fill | fl |
| for | 4 |
| for example | eg |
| forecast | $^f$cst 4cast |
| forename | $^f$nm 4nm |
| foretell | $^f$tl 4tl |
| forewarn | $^f$wrn 4wrn |
| free | fre |
| full | fl |
| fundamentally | fnd$^{my}$ |
| funds | fnds |

| G, H | |
|---|---|
| get | gt |
| give | gv |
| good | gd |
| great | gr8 |
| greater than | > |
| group | grp |
| | |
| had | hd |
| hardship | hrd$^p$ |
| harm | hrm |
| has | hs |
| have | hv |
| he | h |
| helpful | hlp$^f$ |
| her | hr |
| his | hs |
| hours | hrs |
| how | hw |

| I | |
|---|---|
| I | i |
| if | if |
| immediately | immed |
| important | imp |
| improving | imprv$^g$ |
| including | inc$^g$ |
| increase | inc |
| inspire | inspr |
| interim | $^i$m |
| international | $^i$n$^{nl}$ |
| internet | $^i$nt |
| interrupt | $^i$rpt |
| interview | $^i$vw |
| into | in2 |
| introduce | $^i$dc |
| involvement | invl$^m$ |
| is | s |
| it | t |

| J, K, L | |
|---|---|
| joyful | jy$^f$ |
| judge | jj |
| | |
| key | ke |
| know | no |
| knows | nos |
| | |
| lack | lk |
| lasted | lstd |
| leadership | ldr$^p$ |
| less than | < |
| letters | ltrs |
| little | ltl |
| lock | lk |
| lost | lst |
| lot | lt |

| M | |
|---|---|
| mad | md |
| made | mad |
| manage | mnj |
| manager | mnjr |
| market | mkt |
| me | m |
| media | mdia |
| meeting | mtg |
| member | mbr |
| membership | mbr$^p$ |
| minimum | min |
| mission | m$^n$ |
| much | m$_c$ |
| multi-storey | $^m$stry |
| must | mst |
| my | my |

| N, O | |
|---|---|
| new | nw |
| note well | nb |
| number | no |
| ocean | o$^n$ |
| of | f |
| organisation | org |
| organising | org$^g$ |
| other | o$_t$r |
| our | our |

| P | | Q, R, S | |
|---|---|---|---|
| paper | ppr | question | ? |
| pay | pa | | |
| payment | pa$^m$ | | |
| people | ppl | received | rcvd |
| perfect | $^p$fct | recommend | $^{rc}$mnd |
| permit | $^p$mt | relationship | rla$^{np}$ |
| please | pls | replies | rplis |
| plus | + | residential | rsdn$^s$ |
| possible | ps$^b$ | responsible | rspn$^b$ |
| potential | ptn$^s$ | | |
| practice | prctc | | |
| practise | prcts | | |
| prepare | $^p$pr | | |
| probably | $^p$b$^{by}$ | | |
| problems | $^p$blms | | |
| product | $^p$dct | sample | smpl |
| project | $^p$jct | seal | sel |
| promote | $^p$mt | see | c |
| proposal | $^p$psl | sell | sl |
| protect | $^p$tct | service | srvc |
| provide | $^p$vd | she | sh |
| | | shopping | shp$^g$/$_s$p$^g$ |
| | | since | s$^c$ |
| | | skills | skls |
| | | social | so$^s$ |
| | | Spanish | spn$_s$ |
| | | special | sp$^s$ |
| | | specialist | sp$^{st}$ |

| S | |
|---|---|
| speedwriting | s/w |
| station | sta$^n$ |
| stationary | sta$^{ny}$ |
| stationery | sta$^{ny}$ |
| student | stdnt |
| submit | $^s$mt |
| success | scs |
| successfully | scs$^{fy}$ |
| supermarket | $^s$mkt |
| supervision | $^s$v$^n$ |
| support | $^s$prt |
| suppress | $^s$prs |

| T | |
|---|---|
| table | t$^b$ |
| taken | tkn |
| teach | te$_c$ |
| team | tem |
| tell | tl |
| than | tn |
| that | tht |
| that is | ie |
| the | th |
| them | thm |
| then | thn |
| there | thr |
| therefore | ∴ /thr4 |
| these | ths |
| they | thy |
| this | thi |
| those | thos |
| time | tim |
| to | 2 |
| took | tk |
| touch | t$_c$ |
| transcription | $^t$crp$^n$ |
| transfer | $^t$fr |
| translate | $^t$lat |
| transmit | $^t$mt |
| transport | $^t$prt |

| U, V | |
|---|---|
| under | $^u$ |
| underestimate | $^u$est |
| underneath | $^u$nth |
| understand | $^u$stnd |
| useful | us$^f$ |
| value | vlu |
| very | v |
| view | vw |
| visit | vst |
| visiting | vst$^g$ |
| vital | vtl |

| W, X, Y, Z | |
|---|---|
| watch | w$_c$ |
| we | w |
| week | wk |
| were | wr |
| what | wh |
| when | whn |
| where | whr |
| which | w$_c$ |
| while | whl |
| why | y |
| will | wl |
| with | wi |
| within | w/in |
| without | w/ou |
| work | wrk |
| working | wrk$^g$ |
| you | u |

# Universe of
# Learning Books

"The purpose of learning is growth, and our
minds, unlike our bodies, can continue growing
as we continue to live." Mortimer Adler

# About the publishers

Universe of Learning Limited is a small publisher based in the UK with production in England, Australia and America. Our authors are all experienced trainers or teachers who have taught their skills for many years. We are actively seeking qualified authors and if you visit the authors section on www.uolearn.com you can find out how to apply.

If you are interested in any of our current authors (including Heather Baker) coming to speak at your event please do visit their own websites (to contact Heather please email heather@uolearn.com, website www.bakerthompsonassoc.co.uk) or email them through the author section of the uolearn site.

If you would like to purchase larger numbers of books then please do contact us (sales@uolearn.com). We give discounts from 5 books upwards. For larger volumes we can also quote for changes to the cover to accommodate your company logo and to the interior to brand it for your company.

All our books are written by teachers, trainers or people well experienced in their roles and our goal is to help people develop their skills with a well structured range of exercises.

If you have any feedback about this book or other topics that you'd like to see us cover please do contact us at support@uolearn.com.

To buy the printed books please order from your favourite bookshop, including Amazon, Waterstones, Blackwells and Barnes and Noble. For ebooks please visit www.uolearn.com.

*Keep Learning!*

# Successful Business Writing

## How to write excellent and persuasive communications

ISBN 978-1-84937-071-4, from www.uolearn.com

✓ Think about the purpose of the communication
✓ Create successful text for emails, letters, minutes, reports, brochures, websites, and social media
✓ Write effective communications to persuade people
✓ Sample letters and emails
✓ Know how to write good English

# Report Writing

## An easy to follow format for writing reports

ISBN 978-1-84937-036-3, from www.uolearn.com

This book makes report writing a step by step process for you to follow every time you have a report to write.

✓ How to set objectives using 8 simple questions
✓ Easy to follow flow chart
✓ How to write an executive summary
✓ How to layout and structure the report
✓ Help people remember what they read

# Successful Minute Taking Meeting the Challenge

## How to prepare, write and organise agendas and minutes of meetings

ISBN 978-1-84937-040-0, from www.uolearn.com

✓ Becoming more confident in your role
✓ A checklist of what to do
✓ Help with layout and writing skills
✓ Learn what to include in minutes
✓ How to work well with your chairperson

Learn to be an excellent meeting secretary.

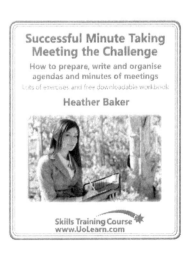

# Studying for your Future

### Skills for life, whilst you study

ISBN: 978-1-84937-047-9, Order at www.uolearn.com

- ✓ A checklist to put together a portfolio
- ✓ Goal setting to help you focus on your future
- ✓ Improve your study skills and exam preparation
- ✓ Prepare for employment

# How to Start a Business as a Private Tutor

ISBN  978-1-84937-029-5, from www.uolearn.com

This book, by a Lancashire based author, shows you how to set up your own business as a tutor.

- ✓ Packed with tips and stories
- ✓ How to get started - what to do and buy
- ✓ How to attract clients and advertise
- ✓ Free printable forms, ready to use

# Dreaming Yourself Aware

### Exercises to interpret your dreams

ISBN: 978-1-84937-055-4, Order at www.uolearn.com

- ✓ Learn how to remember and record your dreams
- ✓ Structured approach to understand your dreams
- ✓ A large variety of techniques for dream interpretation
- ✓ Step by step instructions and worked examples
- ✓ Understand your motivation and reveal your goals

# Developing your assertive communication skills

ISBN: 978-1-84937-082-0, Order at www.uolearn.com

- ✓ Decide what you want and communicate it effectively
- ✓ Develop your confidence
- ✓ Step by step instructions and worked examples to achieve the results you need

# Coaching Skills Training Course

## Business and life coaching techniques for

ISBN: 978-1-84937-019-6, from www.uolearn.com
- ✓ An easy to follow 5 step model
- ✓ Learn to both self-coach and coach others
- ✓ Over 25 ready to use ideas
- ✓ Goal setting tools to help achieve ambitions

A toolbox of ideas to help you become a great coach.

# Stress Management

## Exercises and techniques to manage stress and anxiety

ISBN: 978-1-84937-002-8, from www.uolearn.com
- ✓ Understand what stress is
- ✓ Become proactive in managing your stress
- ✓ How to become more positive about your life
- ✓ An easy 4 step model to lasting change

# Practical and Effective Performance Management

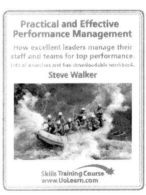

ISBN: 978-1-84937-037-0, from www.uolearn.com
- ✓ Five key ideas to understanding performance
- ✓ A clear four step model
- ✓ Key what works research that is practical
- ✓ A large, wide ranging choice of tools
- ✓ Practical exercises and action planning for managers

A toolbox of ideas to help you become a better leader.

# Developing Your Influencing Skills

ISBN: 978-1-84937-004-2, from www.uolearn.com
- ✓ Decide what your influencing goals are
- ✓ Find ways to increase your credibility rating
- ✓ Develop stronger and more trusting relationships
- ✓ Inspire others to follow your lead
- ✓ Become a more influential communicator

Packed with case studies, exercises and practical tips to become more influential.

"Success will never be a big step in the future,
success is a small step taken just now."
Jonatan Mårtensson

CPSIA information can be obtained at www.ICGtesting.com
Printed in the USA
LVOW111903050613

337140LV00019B/808/P